To our dear Carrie..
Happy 24th Birthday.
Love & Kisses
Dad & Mom.

Soup Beautiful Soup

All human history attests
That happiness for man – the hungry sinner! –
Since Eve ate apples, much depends on dinner.

(Byron – *Don Juan*)

Bon Appétit

bouillon

3 half
chicken
breasts

bay leaf

thyme

Bon Appétit

SOUP, BEAUTIFUL SOUP

A collection of soup recipes
by Ursel Norman
Designed and illustrated by Derek Norman

William Morrow & Company, Inc.

New York

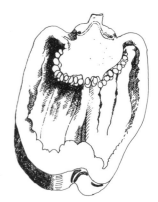

Printed in Great Britain

Library of Congress Catalog Card Number 76–245
ISBN 0-688-03056-4

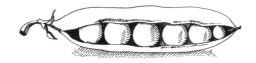

CONTENTS

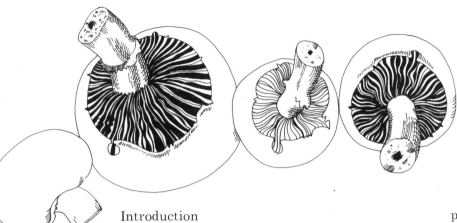

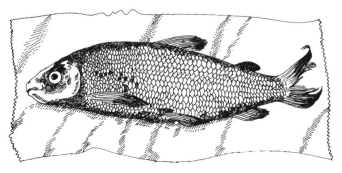

INTRODUCTION

Beautiful Soup! Who cares for fish,
Game, or any other dish?
Who would not give all else for two
pennyworth only of beautiful Soup?
Beau-ootiful Soup!
Beau-ootiful Soup!
Soo-oop of the e-e-evening,
Beautiful, beauti-FUL Soup!

This famed piece from *Alice in Wonderland* by Lewis Carroll is but a taste of the wealth of poetic language that has helped immortalize soup. For centuries soup has given inspiration to peasants and poets and sent gourmets into lyrical raptures.
For soup is a dish to stimulate the imagination and whet the appetite. As one early 20th century gourmet put it: 'There is nothing like a plate of hot soup, its wisp of aromatic steam making the nostrils quiver with anticipation . . . one whiff of a savoury, aromatic soup and appetites come to attention.'
Soup has historically played a highly significant part in man's existence, for it was a basis for nourishment and survival. The cauldron was the original stock-pot and provided an ever changing broth enriched daily with whatever ingredients happened to be available.
Such simple peasant fare gave birth to the earliest of the myriad national soups, many of which fortunately survive.
For every country, there is virtually a national soup. Their preparation is often somewhat similar, but differing by virtue of ingredients, which reflect regional and national tastes.
Some of the most famous are Pot-au-Feu from France, Minestrone from Italy, Borscht from Russia, Gazpacho from Spain and Erwtensoep from Holland.
Within this book you will find all of these soups, together with many more, each with its classic flavor representing some of the finest of European and American cookery. All have their individual tastes, aromas and rich historical associations.
Their different characteristics reflect the gastronomic cultures from which they originate, tastes never to be found in any can, but easily and inexpensively produced within any home kitchen.

Escoffier in his famous *Guide Culinaire* divides soups into two leading classes. 1) 'Clear soups, which include plain and garnished consommés. 2) Thick soups, which comprise the Purées, Veloutés and Creams.' The first class are clear meat or poultry broths, frequently served with some kind of dainty garnish. The second class of soups are made with some kind of starchy ingredient, producing cream soups of various kinds. There is a third type of soup, usually a main-dish soup, like, for instance, Erwtensoep, Minestrone or Gumbo, which are very popular. These fall somewhere in between the first two categories. There are many examples of all three categories within the pages of *Soup, Beautiful Soup*.

It is our sincere hope that the reader will be inspired to make extensive use of the recipes within these pages and that the very thought of homemade soup will send the cook scuttling into the kitchen!

We trust that both the style and content of this book do more than justice to the subject of soups and that the 'Look and Cook' format will prove a useful and practical tool in the kitchen. For it is designed so that the reader can comprehend at a glance how a dish is prepared and how it should look when finally it reaches the table.

Finally, we owe a debt of gratitude and thanks to all our tasters, on both sides of the Atlantic, who have kindly helped us appraise the taste and quality of all the recipes in this book. We hope the reader will find them as tantalizing as we do, proving to be feasts for your eye as well as your palate! For what can be better, or bettered, than:

'Soo-oop of the e-e-evening,
Beautiful, beauti-FUL Soup!'

Soup
Beautiful
Soup

HOW TO MAKE YOUR SOUPS SUPER

Some Do's and Don'ts

Stocks

Almost all the recipes in this book use stock as the cooking liquid. Only when a large amount of meat and bone is used will water do. The best stocks, of course, are the ones you make yourself (recipes page 62). And if you have the time, do try them. The soup can only be as good as the ingredients that you put in – a good stock is half the battle.

However, canned stocks or bouillon cubes can be substituted as long as you remember that the latter are usually highly seasoned. So go carefully on other seasoning, salt especially.

Skimming

Most soups throw up a lot of frothy scum just before they come to a boil. This ought to be skimmed off as best you can. It helps to give the soup a fresh, clear, clean taste and color.

The best skimming tool is a soup ladle. Dip the ladle in a basin of cold water, shake dry, then dip it straight down into the soup (or stock) but *only just* below the surface, and skim off any froth that accumulates at the sides of the pot. Rinse the ladle in the basin with cold water before repeating the process. Further scum will also be thrown against the sides of the pot, so keep skimming just the sides. Skim and rinse until the scum ceases to appear.

Degreasing

Degreasing is done in much the same way as skimming. Only when there is little fat left on the surface, and skimming gets too difficult, can you use a spoon to lift off the remaining "eyes". If you have trouble getting them out, run a paper towel across the surface quickly to mop up some of the grease. No soup – indeed no food – should ever appear on the table with a film of fat on it. One easy way to get it off is to let the soup get cold in the refrigerator. The cold will harden the fat on the surface and you can lift it off easily.

Soup meats

The best meats for soups are those with bones, whether beef, lamb or chicken. These are usually the most inexpensive ones too, and they don't suffer from the long cooking.

Soup Vegetables

Many, many vegetables are used in soup making. But apart from those which give the soup its name and taste, there are the "aromatic" vegetables that appear in almost all soups: onions, carrots and celery. Their flavor is greatly enhanced if they are sautéed in a little butter or margarine before being added.

Soup Pots

A good soup pot is a large, heavy-bottomed aluminium pot with a lid, rather taller than wide, of about a 20-pint (10 quart) capacity. A thin, light aluminium pot with a thin bottom and sides is unsuitable, since it is bound to burn the longer-cooking soups.

If you do not possess such a pot – and they are not cheap – do invest in one. You'll find lots of other uses for it, like cooking pasta or large amounts of greens, corn-on-the-cob, etc.

Covering the Pot

Very frequently in this book you will find the term "partially covered." This means that the lid should be set askew *just* a little, leaving only a tiny crack open. The escape of moisture will be minimal, since most of it will accumulate on the underside of the lid and drop back into the pot. The reason for doing this is to stop the soup from boiling too rapidly – and to stop the lid from rattling. If "uncovered" is mentioned, this is done to concentrate the flavors through evaporation.

Straining

A variety of soups need straining at some point, either to remove certain ingredients or to be made absolutely smooth.

In most cases the use of a fine-mesh strainer is sufficient. If a soup is too thick to pass through, use the back of a soup ladle to push it through. Far easier than stirring it around with a spoon.

In the case of clear broths or consommés, it is necessary to line the strainer with a damp cloth (wrung out in *cold* water). This dampening expands the fibres of the cloth to make it more efficient. This way even the smallest particles are held back.

Good straining cloths are cotton (not synthetic) that are easy to wash and keep clean. (Top of the list are cloth diapers!)

Thickeners

Many soups contain some amount of starchy thickeners. This can be flour, cornflour, rice or other cereal or potatoes. These are all neutral in taste and color.

Puréed soups made from starchy vegetables (peas or beans) contain enough starch already and don't need thickeners.

Use of the Electric Blender

By far the most efficient way of using a blender is with the lid off. This of course is not practical all the time, especially when small children are trying to get a peep at what is going on, but when all is quiet and peaceful, use this method:

With the motor in the off position, pour one soup-ladleful into the blender jar. Turn the blender to the lowest speed. When the contents are smooth, add a second ladleful, then a third. When all this is smooth, turn to the highest speed and keep it there for a minute or two, or until the soup is absolutely smooth. Never do more than 3 ladlefuls at a time; over-filling reduces the efficiency.

If the soup is too thick to be puréed, thin it down with a little of whatever cooking liquid was used in the recipe (stock).

Flavor Enhancers and Food Color

Absolutely none, ever, in anything! Food colors are quite unnecessary anyway. No food needs to look more yellow or more green than nature made it, and correct seasoning eliminate any need for flavor enhancers.

Freezing Soups

Nearly all soups can be frozen without any loss of taste or texture. If it does look lumpy after defrosting, a quick beating with a wire whisk during reheating will restore the smoothness. Guides to which soups can be frozen are included in the recipes.

1 pound of raw lobster meat, fresh or frozen, cut into ½-inch chunks
1 medium carrot, chopped
1 medium onion, chopped
2 parsley stalks, chopped
6 tbsp. butter
½ tsp. dried thyme
1 bayleaf
2 tbsp. brandy
½ cup white wine
2 pints chicken stock or bouillon
⅜ cup long grain rice, uncooked
1 pint water
4 tbsp. unsalted butter
¼ cup heavy cream
cayenne pepper to taste
salt and pepper to taste

Serves 5–6

1   In the soup pot, sauté the chopped onion, carrot and parsley in the butter for 5 minutes. Add the thyme and bayleaf and sauté further until the vegetables just begin to brown.

3   Pour the brandy into a small soup ladle and ignite it by holding it over a gas flame (or use a match). When the brandy is actually burning, pour it over the fish and the vegetables, shaking the pot vigorously until the flame dies down.

4   Then add the wine. Boil the mixture over a high heat until the liquid has reduced to less than half.

5   Add the stock and simmer the bisque, uncovered, for about 10 minutes.

6   Meanwhile, boil the rice in the water till tender (about 20 minutes). Add the rice and water to the soup.

7   Purée the soup in the blender until it is absolutely smooth, first on low speed for a minute, then on high. Strain it through a fine-mesh strainer, pushing it down with the back of a soup ladle. Discard what does not go through. Return soup to pot.

8   Bring the soup to a boil and skim as necessary. Also skim off any fat that rises to the surface. Boil it, uncovered, until the scum no longer appears.

Just before serving, blend in the butter and cream and season to taste with cayenne, salt and pepper.

Brandy

Flame

BUTTER

chopped onion

thyme

bayleaf

LOBSTER MEAT

2   Add the chunks of lobster meat and stir them around with the vegetables until the lobster acquires a nice pink color.

COOKED RICE
& COOKING WATER

stock

return to pot

Strain

Note For Bisque de Crevettes (Shrimp Bisque) substitute 1 pound of shelled shrimp for the lobster meat. (Shrimp will need to be cooked an extra 5–10 minutes at stage 5.) For bisque de Crabe (Crabmeat Bisque) substitute 1 pound of crabmeat for the lobster meat.

Bisque can be made ahead up to stage 7, and even frozen if necessary.

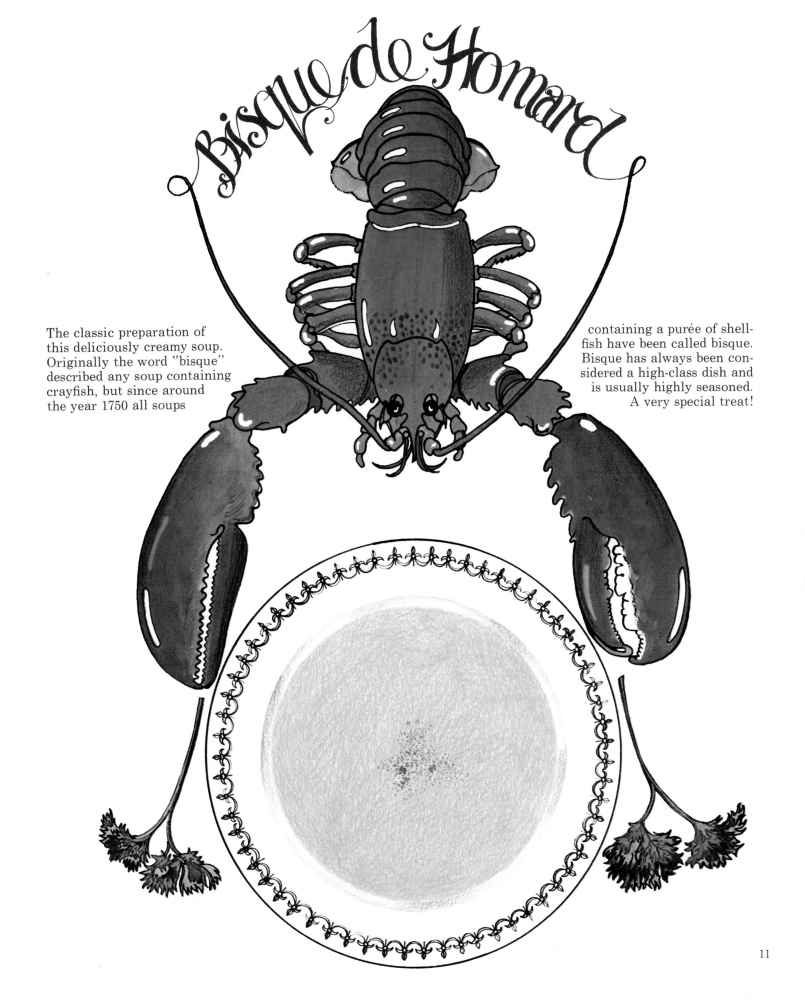

Bisque de Homard

The classic preparation of this deliciously creamy soup. Originally the word "bisque" described any soup containing crayfish, but since around the year 1750 all soups containing a purée of shellfish have been called bisque. Bisque has always been considered a high-class dish and is usually highly seasoned. A very special treat!

2 oz. salt pork *or* **fat bacon, diced very fine**
2 medium onions, finely chopped
3 medium potatoes, diced
½ tsp. dried thyme
1 pint clam juice or water
3 cans (6½ oz. each) minced clams and their liquid *or*
2 dozen finely chopped raw clams and all their liquid plus 1 pint clam juice or water

1 pint rich milk *or* **half-and-half)**
5 tbsp. flour
salt and pepper to taste
finely chopped parsley for garnish
a little paprika for garnish

Serves 6–7

3 Now add the minced or fresh clams and their liquid, and the milk or half-and-half. Simmer, uncovered, about 10 minutes.

4 Mix the flour with enough water to make a pouring consistency. Pour into the boiling soup slowly, stirring all the time with a wire whisk. Simmer, stirring all the time, for 3 minutes. Season to taste with salt and pepper.

Sprinkle with chopped parsley and a dusting of paprika. Traditionally served with crackers.

Note Reheats, but does not freeze.

SALT PORK

finely chopped

3 potatoes peeled & diced

thyme

CLAM JUICE

Milk

Flour

water

season to taste

1 In a large saucepan set over medium heat sauté the salt pork or bacon until it has rendered all its fat and is lightly browned. Add the onions and sauté the mixture until the onions are soft and transparent.

2 Add the potatoes, thyme and clam juice or water, and simmer, uncovered, until the potatoes are cooked but not falling apart.

NEW ENGLAND CLAM CHOWDER

The name chowder is derived from the French *chaudière* (literally meaning the fish kettle in which the dish was cooked) and was probably anglicized subsequent to the French settling in Canada. New England Clam Chowder is by far the most distinguished of all the clam chowders, with its characteristic clams, salt pork and milk or cream. Herman Melville immortalized the dish in his salty classic, *Moby Dick*. 'Oh! sweet friends, harken to me. It was made of small juicy clams, scarcely bigger than hazelnuts, mixed with pounded ships biscuits, and salted pork cut up into little flakes, the whole enriched with butter and plentifully seasoned with pepper and salt.' The recipe here you will find a little more reliable, though guaranteed to rouse similar feelings of delight. We feel sure Herman Melville would have approved.

2 pounds fresh tomatoes, peeled and chopped, *or* one 2-pound can tomatoes, chopped
2 large onions, chopped
4–8 cloves garlic, crushed
2 sprigs parsley
1 bayleaf
1 tsp. dried thyme
4–5 fennel seeds
2 pinches saffron
1 fresh or frozen lobster tail (shell left on and cut vertically into 2-inch slices)
3 pounds various firm fish, cut into serving pieces (leaving the skin on some adds color). Choose from: halibut, pike, cod, haddock or red snapper
1 cup olive oil
1 tsp. pepper
2 tsp. salt

11 cups liquid, either cold water *or* ⅔ water and ⅓ white wine *or* fish stock from page 62
3 pounds various soft fish, cut into serving pieces (leave the skin on some). Choose from: mackerel, whiting, whitefish, flounder, sole, mullet or perch
12 croûtons (optional). These are slices of French bread, brushed with oil on both sides and toasted in a 325° oven till crisp and dry

Serves 10–12

1 Place the tomatoes, their juice, onion, garlic, parsley, bayleaf, thyme, fennel seeds and saffron into large soup pot.

2 On the bed of vegetables and herbs place the cut up lobster tail and all the pieces of firm fish. Pour over this the olive oil, 1 teaspoon pepper and 2 teaspoons salt.

3 Cover the fish and vegetables with the liquid. Bring to a boil over very high heat. Continue boiling rapidly (do *not* turn down the heat), uncovered, for 7–8 minutes.

fennel seeds

LOBSTER TAIL

FIRM FISH

wine optional

thyme

SOFT FISH

water & wine (or fish stock)

4 Now add all the soft fish. Continue boiling on high heat another 7 minutes. Taste for seasoning.

5 To serve: Using a slotted spoon, transfer all the fish to a platter. Serve the broth in deep soup plates. Pass the fish separately. (If croûtons are used, place one in each soup plate first, then spoon the broth on top, then the fish.)

Note *Do not freeze!* This soup can be reheated – with a minimum of stirring so as not to break up the fish.

BOUILLABAISSE

In his poem 'The Ballad of Bouillabaisse,' William Thackery has helped immortalize this hearty Mediterranean dish. Bouillabaisse is generally recognized as having originated in Marseilles, although many areas in Provence claim to make the genuine Bouillabaisse. Try this Marseillaise Bouillabaisse, great with good company and hearty conversation. The Parisian version would also include mussels or clams. A rich spicy main-dish soup.

5 cups rich chicken stock or bouillon

¼ cup long-grain rice, uncooked

2 whole eggs *or* **1 egg and 2 egg yolks**

juice of 1 lemon

a little salt (if needed)

Serves 4–5

3 With a wire whisk stir this mixture into the soup, and stirring constantly let it only *just* come to a boil. Remove from heat immediately.

1 Heat the chicken stock to boiling point. Slowly stir in the rice and simmer, partially covered, until the rice is tender (15–20 minutes).

Season with salt if necessary.

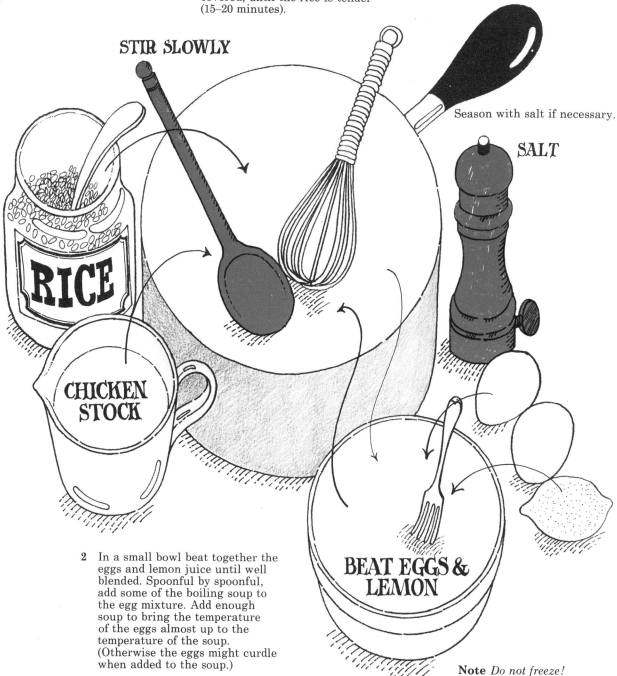

STIR SLOWLY

SALT

RICE

CHICKEN STOCK

BEAT EGGS & LEMON

2 In a small bowl beat together the eggs and lemon juice until well blended. Spoonful by spoonful, add some of the boiling soup to the egg mixture. Add enough soup to bring the temperature of the eggs almost up to the temperature of the soup. (Otherwise the eggs might curdle when added to the soup.)

Note *Do not freeze!*

GREEK AUGOLÉMONO

The best known of Greek soups. Simple ingredients are combined to create a fragrant tangy flavor.

½ pound dry white beans, washed
5 tbsp. oil
1 large onion, cut into neat cubes
1 stalk celery, cut into neat cubes
2 or more cloves garlic, crushed
3 medium carrots, cut into neat cubes
8 oz. fresh or frozen peas
½ pound unpeeled zucchini
   (cut into neat cubes)
2 leeks, chopped (if available)
½ pound cabbage, shredded
½ tsp. dried rosemary
2 oz. salt pork or streaky bacon, cubed
1 pound fresh tomatoes, peeled and
   chopped or one 16-oz. can tomatoes,
   roughly chopped

4 pints beef stock or bouillon
1 bayleaf
2 parsley sprigs } tied together
salt and pepper to taste
½ cup uncooked rice or 4 oz. soup
   noodles
5 tbsp. grated parmesan cheese

Serves 10

1 Soak the beans overnight in enough water to cover.

2 Cook the beans, covered, in the soaking water until tender, about 1–1½ hours. Add a little more water if they become too dry. Drain and reserve.

drain

3 Meanwhile, heat the oil in a heavy frying pan. In it sauté the onion, celery, garlic, carrot, fresh peas (if peas are frozen, add them later), zucchini, leeks and cabbage. Sauté them, stirring often, for 10 minutes. Stir in the rosemary. Remove from pan and reserve.

SAUTÉ

ROSEMARY

oil

4 Sauté the diced salt pork or bacon in the same frying pan till crisp and brown. Drain on paper towel and reserve.

Sauté until crisp & brown

salt pork

drain

5 Into a large pot place the sautéed vegetables. Stir in the tomatoes, beef stock, bayleaf and parsley. Bring to a boil and simmer, partially covered, for about 20 minutes.

stock

skinned & chopped

6 Add the rice or noodles, reserved beans and pork, and the peas (if frozen). Simmer, partially covered, 15–20 minutes longer. Discard bayleaf and parsley. Taste for seasoning.

Pass the grated parmesan separately.

Note Reheats and freezes well.

Minestrone alla Milanese

An Italian classic with numerous regional variations. This particular recipe is a typical Milanese version, using rice as the thickener. Minestrone is to Italy what Pot au Feu is to France – it contains all the natural goodness and nutrition of fresh vegetables to give a hearty main-dish soup.

1   Cover the leeks with cold water and sprinkle some salt over them. Leave to soak for 20 minutes or so. Rinse well; leeks are usually very sandy.

1½ pounds fresh leeks, sliced ¼-inch thick
about 2 tsp. salt
1 small chicken
3 cups chicken stock or bouillon
3 parsley sprigs ⎫
1 bay leaf   ⎬ tied together
½ tsp. dried thyme
⅓ cup pearl barley
1 cup heavy cream (or to taste)
salt and pepper to taste
chopped parsley for garnish

Serves 4

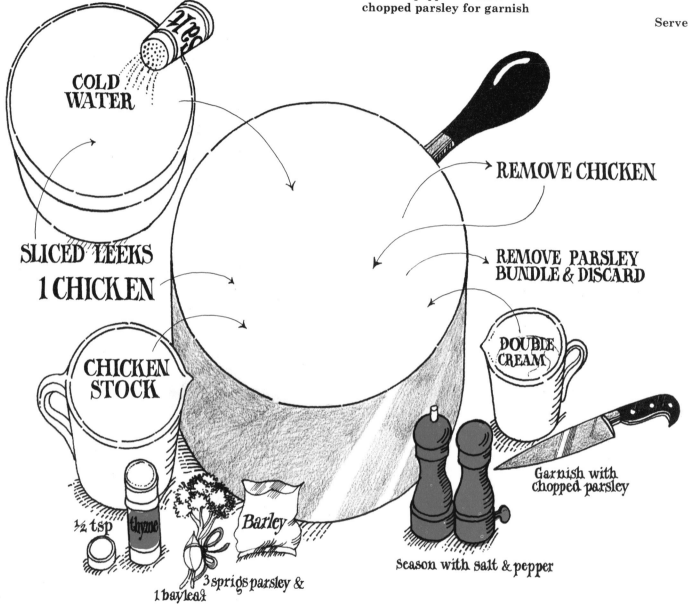

COLD WATER

SLICED LEEKS
1 CHICKEN

REMOVE CHICKEN

REMOVE PARSLEY BUNDLE & DISCARD

DOUBLE CREAM

CHICKEN STOCK

½ tsp thyme

3 sprigs parsley &
1 bay leaf

Barley

Season with salt & pepper

Garnish with chopped parsley

2   Put the chicken into a large soup pot. Add the stock or bouillon, parsley/bayleaf bundle, thyme and barley. Simmer the soup, partially covered, for about 40 minutes. Then add the sliced leeks and cook another 15 minutes or so, until the barley is tender.

3   Remove the chicken and reserve. Lift out the parsley bundle and discard. When cool enough to handle, skin and bone the chicken carefully and cut the meat into bite-size pieces. Return meat to soup pot and heat through again.

4   Off the heat, stir in the cream, and season well with salt and pepper. Reheat to just below boiling point. Garnish with chopped parsley.

Note This soup can be made ahead of time and reheated (or frozen) up to stage 3.
(If liked, the soup can be bound with a little cornstarch and water mixture at stage 4.)

COCK~A~LEEKIE

As the name suggests, this soup was originally made with a cockerel.
Nowadays a chicken is more than an adequate substitute. A hearty
main-dish soup – absolutely delight-
ful on a cold winter's day, with
good conversation and
warm, crusty bread.

See! the smoking bowl before us,
Mark our jovial ragged ring!
Round and round take up the chorus,
And in raptures let us sing.
R. Burns

Potage Crécy (Cream of Carrot)
1 pound carrots, roughly chopped
1 large onion, roughly chopped
2 tbsp. butter or margarine
2½ cups chicken stock or bouillon
1 oz. raw rice
salt and pepper to taste
1 egg yolk
¾ cup light cream (*or* half-and-half)
chopped parsley *or* chives for
   garnish   **Serves 4**

1 Sauté the chopped carrots and onion over medium heat in the butter for 5 minutes, stirring frequently.

3 Put soup into blender jar and purée on low speed for a minute. Then turn to high speed until the soup is really smooth. (If the soup should be too thick for puréeing, add a little extra stock.) Strain through a fine-mesh strainer.

4 Return to pot and bring back to boil. Mix egg yolk into the cream and, stirring briskly with a wire whisk, stir it into the soup. Let it bubble up once or twice, then remove from heat immediately. *Do not boil again.*

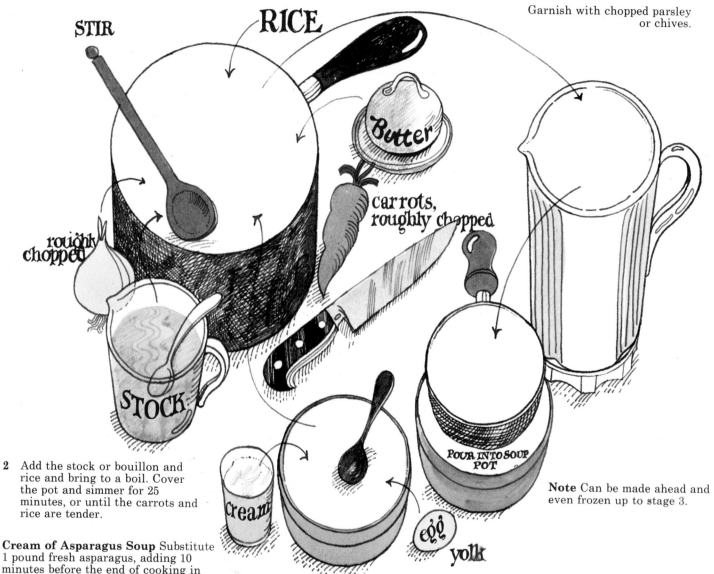

STIR   RICE

Garnish with chopped parsley or chives.

Butter

roughly chopped

carrots, roughly chopped

STOCK

cream

POUR INTO SOUP POT

egg yolk

2 Add the stock or bouillon and rice and bring to a boil. Cover the pot and simmer for 25 minutes, or until the carrots and rice are tender.

Note Can be made ahead and even frozen up to stage 3.

Cream of Asparagus Soup Substitute 1 pound fresh asparagus, adding 10 minutes before the end of cooking in stage 2. (The tips can be poached separately for 5 minutes and added to the soup for garnish.)
Cream of Celery Soup Substitute 1 bunch of celery at stage 1.
Cream of Turnip Substitute 1 pound of turnips at stage 1. (Some leaves can be poached for 5 minutes and added as garnish.)
Cream of Kohlrabi Substitute 1 pound of kohlrabi at stage 1. (Some leaves can be poached for 5 minutes and added as garnish.)

Cream of Celery Root Substitute 1 cubed celery root at stage 1.
Cream of Spinach Substitute 1 pound fresh or frozen spinach leaves 10 minutes before the end of cooking time in stage 2. (Traditional garnish is hardboiled-egg slices.)
Cream of Broccoli Substitute 1 pound fresh broccoli 10 minutes before the end of cooking time in stage 2.
Cream of Cauliflower Substitute 1 pound fresh cauliflower 15 minutes

before the end of cooking time in stage 2. (A few leaves, blanched for 5 minutes, make a nice garnish.)
Cream of Fresh Peas and Lettuce Substitute 1 pound shelled peas and 1 roughly chopped head of Boston lettuce 15 minutes before end of cooking time in stage 2.
Cream of Brussels Sprouts Substitute 1 pound fresh brussels sprouts 15 minutes before the end of cooking time in stage 2.

Spinach Soup
A magnificent taste of spinach that would make Popeye proud! Fresh, appetizing color.

Celery Soup
A fresh vegetable soup that can be enjoyed all year round.

Potage Crécy
A simple, basic recipe that allows for all kinds of variations. Potage Crécy has a delightful orange color, is mildly sweet and very creamy.

Asparagus Soup
Delightful – hot *or* cold!

Kohlrabi Soup
A creamy soup, with a delicate taste and texture. Very good hot *or* cold!

1½–2 pounds beef for soup (chuck neck bones are good to add)
4 pints beef stock or bouillon
1 pound pole beans, sliced diagonally
1 large potato, peeled and cubed
1 onion, chopped
1 carrot, chopped
salt and pepper to taste

Serves 6–8

1 Place the meat in a large soup pot. Pour on the stock. Bring to a boil and skim off any scum that rises to the surface. Add onion and carrot and simmer, partially covered, for 1 hour.

2 Remove the meat and leave to cool slightly.

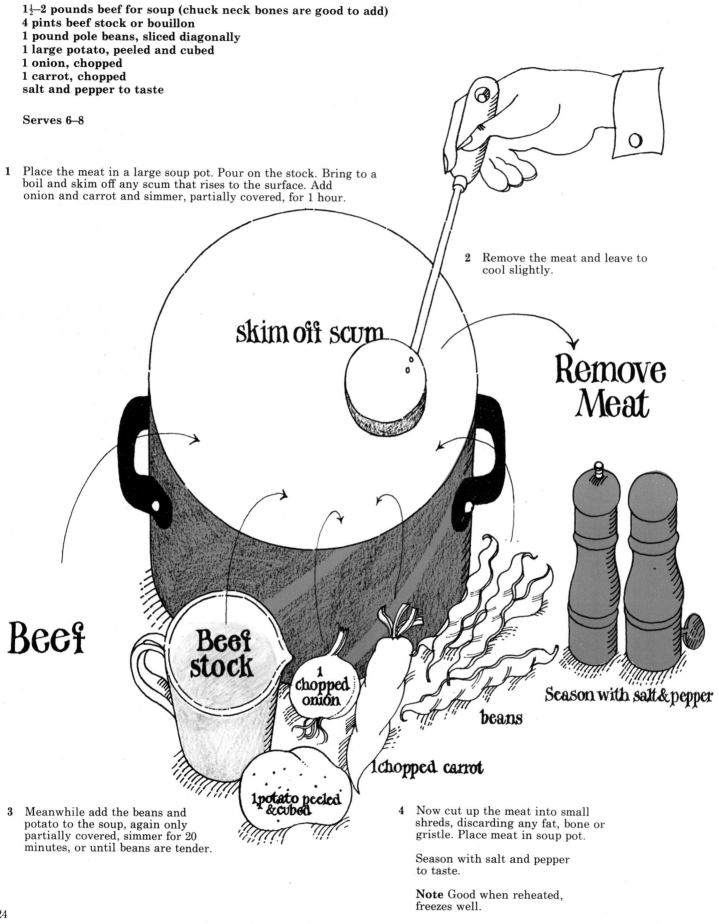

skim off scum

Remove Meat

Beef

Beef stock

1 chopped onion

1 potato peeled & cubed

1 chopped carrot

beans

Season with salt & pepper

3 Meanwhile add the beans and potato to the soup, again only partially covered, simmer for 20 minutes, or until beans are tender.

4 Now cut up the meat into small shreds, discarding any fat, bone or gristle. Place meat in soup pot.

Season with salt and pepper to taste.

Note Good when reheated, freezes well.

Bohnensuppe

A Westphalian soup that oozes a country earthiness. Honest and sincere, extremely low in calories, and full of nutrition. Serve it piping hot for a fine lunch. A meal in itself, especially with crusty bread. Guten Appetit.

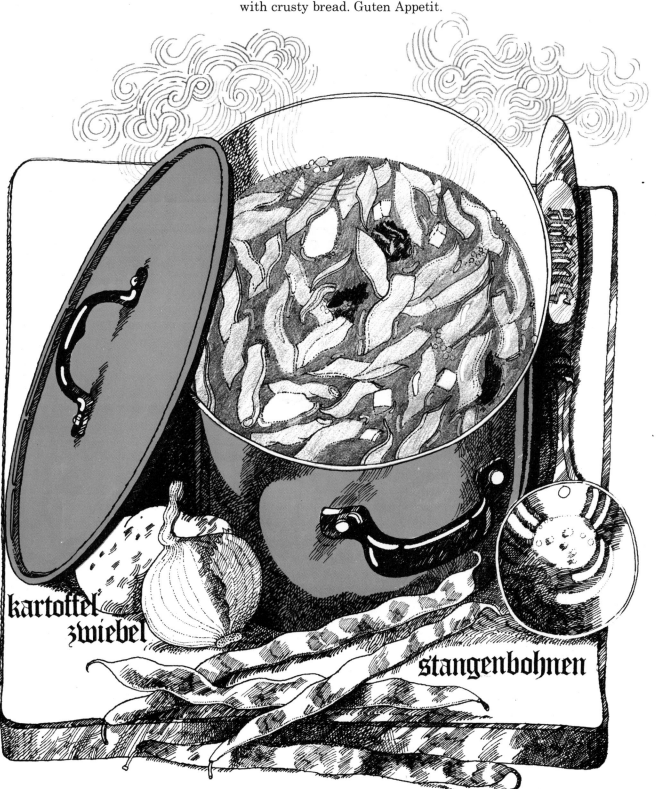

kartoffel

zwiebel

stangenbohnen

2½ pounds fresh tomatoes, peeled and chopped
1 small, peeled and chopped cucumber
1 clove garlic, crushed
1 green pepper, cut into strips
2 tbsp. tomato purée
1 large parsley sprig
¾ cup cold water
4 tbsp. oil
2 tbsp. white wine vinegar
salt and pepper to taste
2 slices ordinary white bread, crust removed, cubed
2 finely sliced green (spring) onions ⎫
1 stalk celery, very finely chopped ⎬ for garnish
a few black olives ⎭

Serves 6

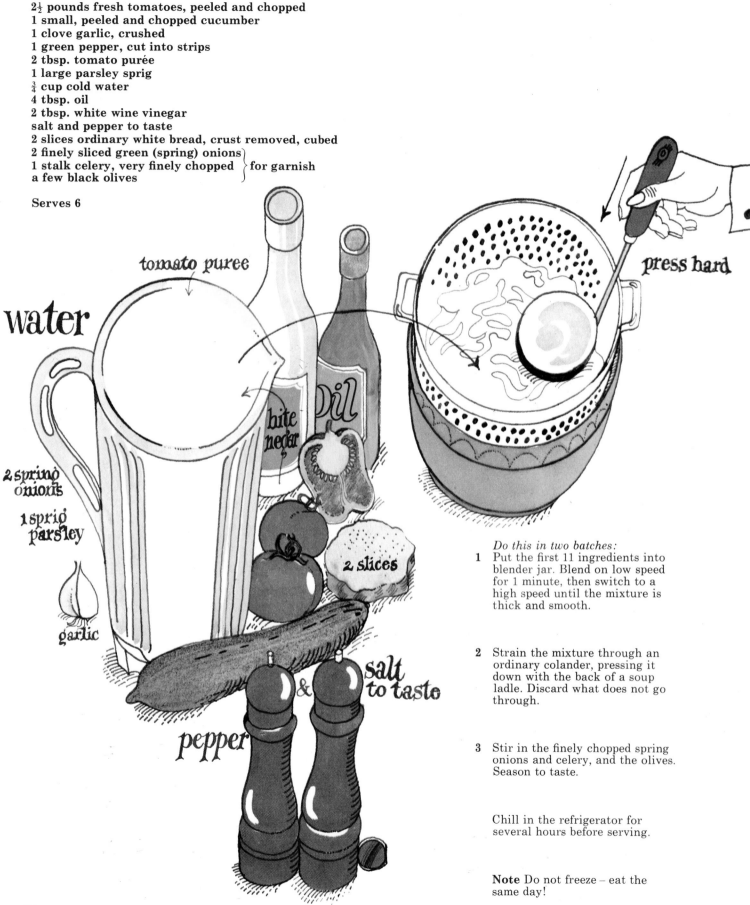

Do this in two batches:

1 Put the first 11 ingredients into blender jar. Blend on low speed for 1 minute, then switch to a high speed until the mixture is thick and smooth.

2 Strain the mixture through an ordinary colander, pressing it down with the back of a soup ladle. Discard what does not go through.

3 Stir in the finely chopped spring onions and celery, and the olives. Season to taste.

Chill in the refrigerator for several hours before serving.

Note Do not freeze – eat the same day!

SPANISH GAZPACHO

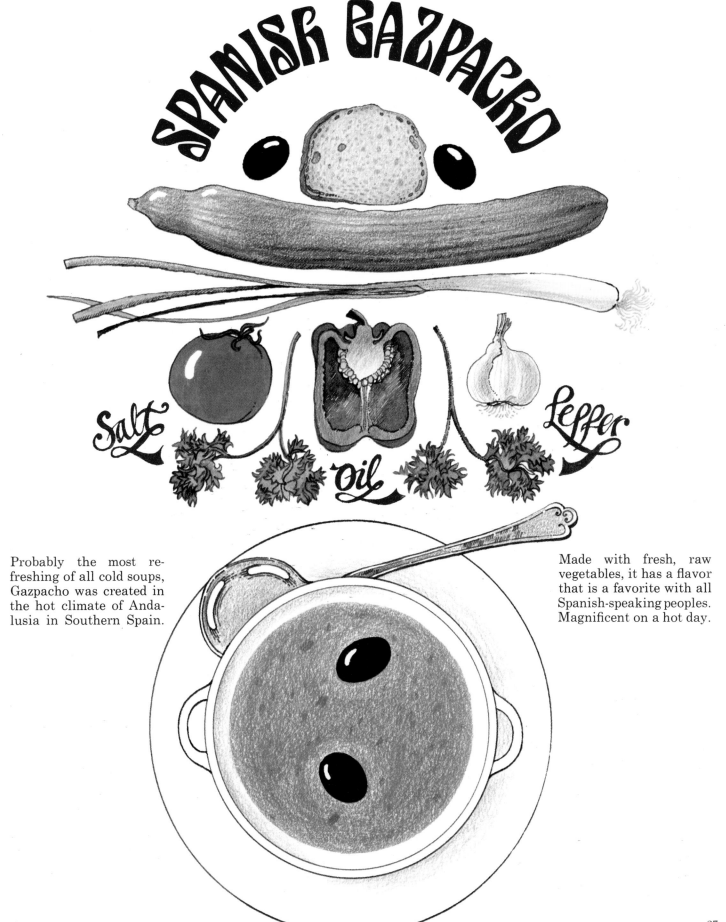

Salt   Oil   Pepper

Probably the most re-
freshing of all cold soups,
Gazpacho was created in
the hot climate of Anda-
lusia in Southern Spain.

Made with fresh, raw
vegetables, it has a flavor
that is a favorite with all
Spanish-speaking peoples.
Magnificent on a hot day.

2 pounds leeks, white part only, sliced
½ pound raw, peeled potato, cubed
3 tbsp. butter
5 cups chicken stock or bouillon
½ cup heavy cream
salt and pepper to taste
chopped chives or parsley for garnish
Serves 5–6

1　Soak the sliced leeks in salted water for 20 minutes. Rinse and drain well.

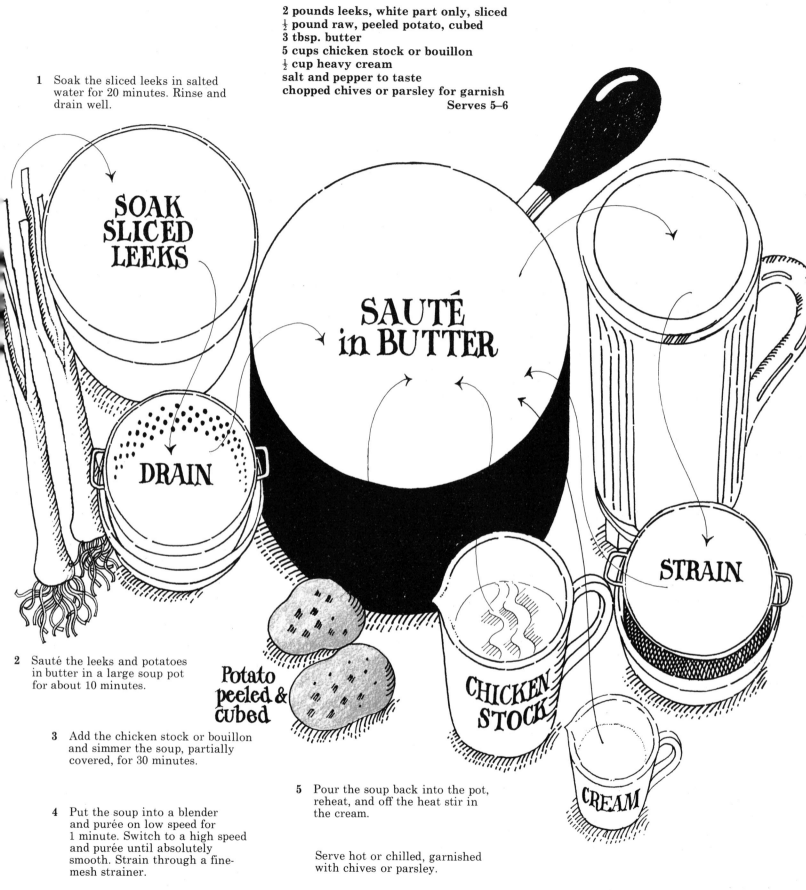

2　Sauté the leeks and potatoes in butter in a large soup pot for about 10 minutes.

3　Add the chicken stock or bouillon and simmer the soup, partially covered, for 30 minutes.

4　Put the soup into a blender and purée on low speed for 1 minute. Switch to a high speed and purée until absolutely smooth. Strain through a fine-mesh strainer.

5　Pour the soup back into the pot, reheat, and off the heat stir in the cream.

Serve hot or chilled, garnished with chives or parsley.

Note The soup can be made ahead and reheated or frozen up to stage 4.

Vichyssoise

Vichyssoise is a beautiful soup of fresh leeks and potatoes, and is only served cold. There is no need here to do as Edward Lear's Young Lady of Poole did,

"whose soup was excessively cool,
so she put it to boil by the aid of some oil,
That ingenious young lady of Poole!"

(If Vichyssoise is served hot, it becomes Potage Crème de Poireaux.) Vichyssoise makes a fine, elegant soup for a formal occasion. Very delicate in taste and texture. Bon Appétit!

for the consommé
5–6 egg whites
2 tsp. salt
½ tsp. pepper
4 cloves
2 pounds very, very lean ground beef (the meat should be from an old animal; young ones yield very little flavor)
1 cup red wine (optional)
8 cups beef stock

Serves 6–8

for the royale
4 parsley sprigs
little salt and pepper
5 fl. oz. consommé or chicken bouillon
1 egg
2 egg yolks

3 To the meat mixture add the cold beef stock and then pour the mixture into a saucepan.

4 Bring to a boil, and simmer (uncovered) very slowly for 1½ to 2 hours, *never* stirring. The liquid must simmer very gently, not come bubbling through the meat mixture. Cook until the cake that has formed on the surface is quite cooked, with no traces of red.

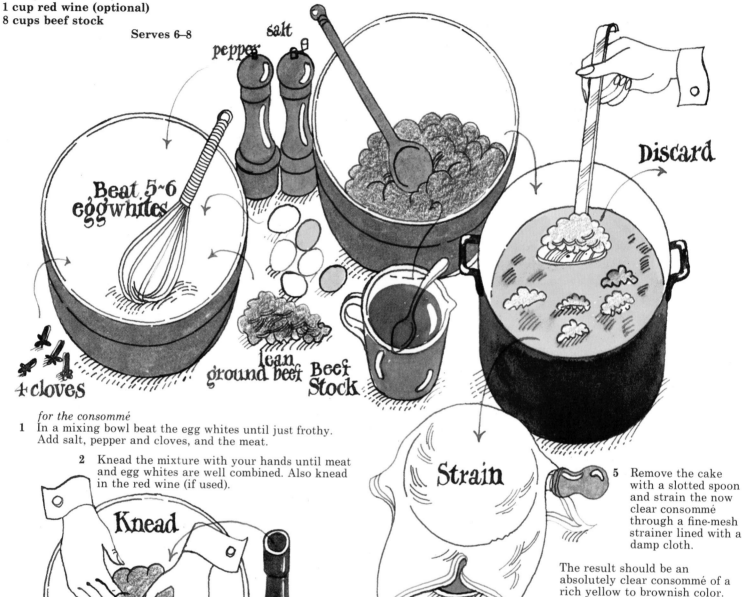

for the consommé

1 In a mixing bowl beat the egg whites until just frothy. Add salt, pepper and cloves, and the meat.

2 Knead the mixture with your hands until meat and egg whites are well combined. Also knead in the red wine (if used).

5 Remove the cake with a slotted spoon and strain the now clear consommé through a fine-mesh strainer lined with a damp cloth.

The result should be an absolutely clear consommé of a rich yellow to brownish color.

Garnish with royale, which should be very neatly stamped into fancy shapes.

for the royale
Simmer the parsley, salt and pepper in the stock for 5 minutes. Cool and remove the parsley. Beat the egg and egg yolks well and add them to the cool stock. Strain the mixture through a fine-mesh strainer. Pour the mixture into a buttered ovenproof flat dish (the mixture should be about ¼ inch deep). Skim off any foam that might form on the surface.
Fill a baking tray with boiling water and set the ovenproof dish into it. Place in a preheated 325° oven for 20 minutes. (Test for doneness with a knife; if it comes out clean, the royale is cooked.) Cool in the dish before cutting.

Other garnishes for consommés
All garnishes for consommés have to be cooked separately, well drained and rinsed to keep them absolutely clean, julienned vegetables blanched 1 minute and rinsed, rice or noodles cooked till tender and rinsed, leftover roast or boiled meat cut into julienne strips, quenelles or profiteroles.

Consommé à la Royale

The word "consommé" literally means a perfectly refined soup. This recipe is a basic consommé, garnished with 'royale.' There are numerous variations of this recipe, each largely differentiated by the type of garnish. Escoffier lists over 70 different kinds. Consommé, it is worth remembering, represents perfection, pure and exquisite. No rustic country character here. Beautifully clear, it stimulates the appetite as no other soup can. Perfect for formal occasions. A triumph of haute cuisine. Bon Appétit.

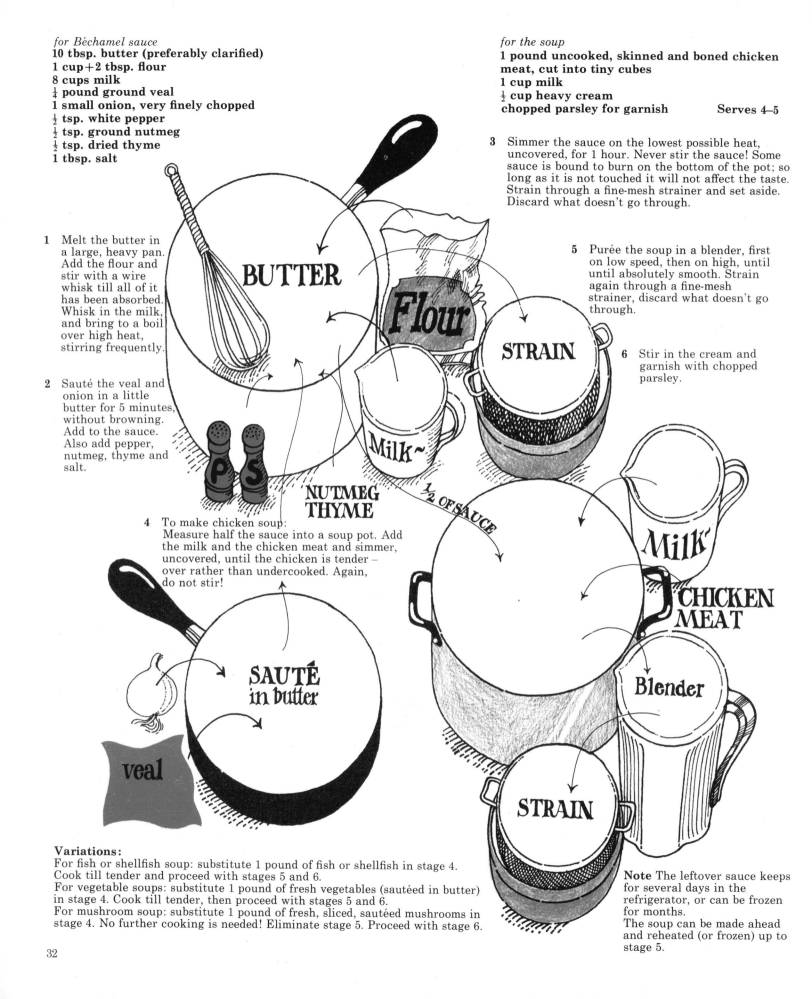

for *Béchamel sauce*
10 tbsp. butter (preferably clarified)
1 cup + 2 tbsp. flour
8 cups milk
¼ pound ground veal
1 small onion, very finely chopped
½ tsp. white pepper
½ tsp. ground nutmeg
½ tsp. dried thyme
1 tbsp. salt

for *the soup*
1 pound uncooked, skinned and boned chicken meat, cut into tiny cubes
1 cup milk
½ cup heavy cream
chopped parsley for garnish   Serves 4–5

1 Melt the butter in a large, heavy pan. Add the flour and stir with a wire whisk till all of it has been absorbed. Whisk in the milk, and bring to a boil over high heat, stirring frequently.

2 Sauté the veal and onion in a little butter for 5 minutes, without browning. Add to the sauce. Also add pepper, nutmeg, thyme and salt.

3 Simmer the sauce on the lowest possible heat, uncovered, for 1 hour. Never stir the sauce! Some sauce is bound to burn on the bottom of the pot; so long as it is not touched it will not affect the taste. Strain through a fine-mesh strainer and set aside. Discard what doesn't go through.

4 To make chicken soup:
Measure half the sauce into a soup pot. Add the milk and the chicken meat and simmer, uncovered, until the chicken is tender – over rather than undercooked. Again, do not stir!

5 Purée the soup in a blender, first on low speed, then on high, until until absolutely smooth. Strain again through a fine-mesh strainer, discard what doesn't go through.

6 Stir in the cream and garnish with chopped parsley.

Variations:
For fish or shellfish soup: substitute 1 pound of fish or shellfish in stage 4. Cook till tender and proceed with stages 5 and 6.
For vegetable soups: substitute 1 pound of fresh vegetables (sautéed in butter) in stage 4. Cook till tender, then proceed with stages 5 and 6.
For mushroom soup: substitute 1 pound of fresh, sliced, sautéed mushrooms in stage 4. No further cooking is needed! Eliminate stage 5. Proceed with stage 6.

Note The leftover sauce keeps for several days in the refrigerator, or can be frozen for months.
The soup can be made ahead and reheated (or frozen) up to stage 5.

CRÈME DE VOLAILLE

Chicken

BRUSSELS SPROUT

Bon Appétit

This is the classic recipe for cream soup of any type. It is based on the extremely versatile Béchamel Sauce, and since it is a little time consuming to prepare, a double recipe for sauce has been given.
This recipe makes a sinfully rich soup – absolutely the creamiest you will ever taste!

4 tbsp. butter
**1 pound onions, cut into thin
    rings**
**1 clove garlic, crushed
    (optional)**
2 tsp. sugar
3 tbsp. flour
**7 cups beef or chicken stock,
    or bouillon**
5 fl. oz. white wine
1 tsp. dried thyme
1 bayleaf
2 tbsp. dry sherry
8 slices French bread
**1 cup grated Swiss or
    parmesan cheese   Serves 8**

1   Melt the butter in a heavy
    saucepan. Add the sliced onion
    and chopped garlic. Sauté,
    covered, over a fairly low heat,
    for 20 minutes. Stir once in a
    while with a wooden spoon.

2   Uncover the pot, raise the heat a
    little and add the sugar. Cook
    for 10 minutes, stirring now and
    then. (The idea is *not* to let the
    sugar burn, just to caramelize it
    to give the soup a rich color.)

3   Sprinkle the flour over the
    onions. Stir it around well.

4   Add the stock to the pot, also the
    wine, thyme and bayleaf. Bring
    to a boil, skimming off any scum
    that rises to the surface.
    Partially cover the pot and
    simmer the soup for 30
    minutes.

5   Just before serving, add the
    sherry.

The garnish;
Cut the bread into 1-inch-thick
slices and toast them on a baking
sheet in a 325° oven about 30
minutes, until they are
completely dry. (Rub them with a
cut clove of garlic after 15
minutes if desired.)
Place a piece of toast onto each
bowl of soup. Sprinkle some
grated cheese on top of each, and
place the bowls under the
broiler for a few minutes to
brown the cheese slightly.

skim off
scum

Butter

sliced onion
chopped garlic

Sugar

Flour

thyme

bayleaf

STOCK

White
Wine

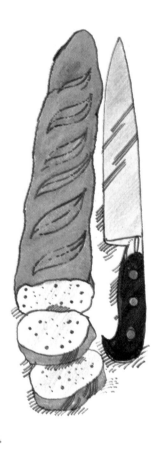

Sher

Note Onion Soup can be made
ahead and frozen up to stage 4.

34

SOUPE À L'OIGNON GRATINÉE

The French Onion Seller

Onion Soup is generally considered French, though why exactly is uncertain. Every country has some form of onion soup, not too different one from another. This heartwarming, juicy soup has enjoyed centuries of popularity. Maybe your appreciation will more than equal Monsieur Bovary's, who in Gustave Flaubert's *Madame Bovary* returns home to find that "For dinner there was onion soup . . . and rubbed his hands together in satisfaction and said cheerfully, 'It is good to be home again!' "

2 tbsp. oil
1–2 pounds lamb for boiling (some nice bones
   included) in one piece
11 cups beef stock or bouillon
1 large onion, chopped
3 medium carrots, chopped
2 stalks celery, chopped
3 tbsp. butter
1 tsp. dried thyme
1 bayleaf
¼ cup pearl barley
4 oz. fresh or frozen peas
salt and pepper to taste

Serves 8–10

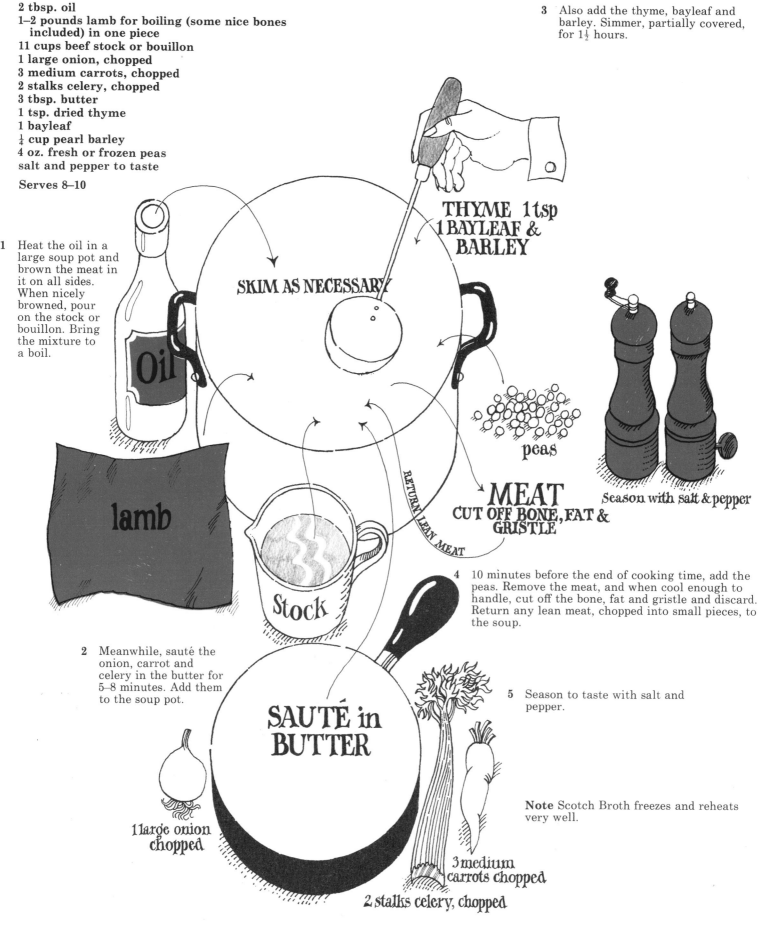

1 Heat the oil in a large soup pot and brown the meat in it on all sides. When nicely browned, pour on the stock or bouillon. Bring the mixture to a boil.

2 Meanwhile, sauté the onion, carrot and celery in the butter for 5–8 minutes. Add them to the soup pot.

3 Also add the thyme, bayleaf and barley. Simmer, partially covered, for 1½ hours.

4 10 minutes before the end of cooking time, add the peas. Remove the meat, and when cool enough to handle, cut off the bone, fat and gristle and discard. Return any lean meat, chopped into small pieces, to the soup.

5 Season to taste with salt and pepper.

Note Scotch Broth freezes and reheats very well.

SKIM AS NECESSARY

THYME 1tsp 1 BAYLEAF & BARLEY

peas

MEAT CUT OFF BONE, FAT & GRISTLE

RETURN LEAN MEAT

Season with salt & pepper

Oil

lamb

Stock

SAUTÉ in BUTTER

1 large onion chopped

3 medium carrots chopped

2 stalks celery, chopped

SCOTCH BROTH

A beautiful soup, hearty, hale and healthy, a basic soup that has its origin in simple country fare. Dr. Johnson gave recognition to the dish on his tour of Scotland in 1773. Try it on a cold, frosty day, in front of the fire.

1–1½ pounds smoked pork hocks *or* a
ham bone with some meat
10 cups cold water
1 medium carrot, finely chopped
1 medium onion, finely chopped
3 tbsp. butter or margarine
1 pound dried split green peas
salt, pepper and nutmeg to taste
chicken stock or bouillon as needed

Serves 6

SMOKED PORK HOCKS

SKIM OFF THE SCUM

1 Place the meat in a large pot and add the cold water. Bring to boil, cover, and simmer until the meat is tender (2 hours for pork hocks, 1 hour for ham bone).

WATER

2 Meanwhile, sauté the carrot and onion in the butter for 5 minutes.

BUTTER

finely chopped

finely chopped

3 When the meat is tender, add the vegetables to the soup pot. Also add the washed peas. Simmer the soup, uncovered, for 20–30 minutes, or until the peas are tender. Skim the soup several times if necessary.

4 Remove the meat from the pot and leave to cool a little. Then cut any lean meat off the bone and cut it into tiny shreds. Discard bone, fat and gristle.

SMOKED PORK HOCKS

5 Purée the soup in a blender, first on low speed, then turn to high until the soup is absolutely smooth.

6 Return the soup to soup pot. Bring back to a boil and simmer a few more minutes. Skim off the scum as it appears. Add the meat.

7 If the soup is too thick at this point, thin it down with chicken stock or bouillon to the desired consistency.

Season to taste with salt, pepper and nutmeg.

Note Excellent reheated, and freezes well.

Variations: Instead of the split green peas, use: 1 pound lentils; 1 pound kidney beans; 1 pound black beans (soak these overnight); 1 pound navy beans; 1 pound split yellow peas; or 1 pound dried lima beans.

ERWTENSOEP

Erwtensoep (Split Pea Soup)
An old-fashioned Dutch soup, full of wholesome goodness and country character. It ranks as one of the most famous of all soups – and one of the oldest. Ideal for lunch or a hearty gathering of friends. An excellent source of protein.

Yellow Pea Soup
Peas are one of the most nutritious of vegetables and have been a source of protein since the beginning of recorded history. Yellow Pea Soup is a magnificent variation of Erwtensoep, rich and golden.

Black Bean Soup
Black beans are cultivated in the southern United States. They make an especially rich and excellent soup, typical of the South. Beans historically have played an important role in man's diet. 'Full of beans' was an apt and descriptive way of describing the state of health and natural good spirits derived from eating beans.
Garnishes for Black Bean Soup are traditionally hardboiled-egg slices and lemon.

2 tbsp. oil
3 large onions, roughly chopped
1–3 cloves garlic, crushed (optional)
3–4 level tablespoons paprika
2 tbsp. oil
1½ pounds lean braising (chuck) steak,
   cut into 1-inch cubes
3 medium carrots, chopped
1 pound tomatoes, peeled and roughly
   chopped or 1 can (16 oz.) tomatoes with
   their liquid
5 cups beef stock or bouillon
2 large potatoes, cubed
½ tsp. caraway seeds
½ tsp. dried marjoram
1 bayleaf
salt and pepper to taste
chopped parsley for
   garnish

      Serves 4–5

1 In a large saucepan sauté the onion in the oil until soft and transparent. Add the garlic, if used, and sauté 1 minute longer.

2 Off the heat (when the bubbling has subsided), add the paprika. Stir until all the onions are coated with it. Set aside.

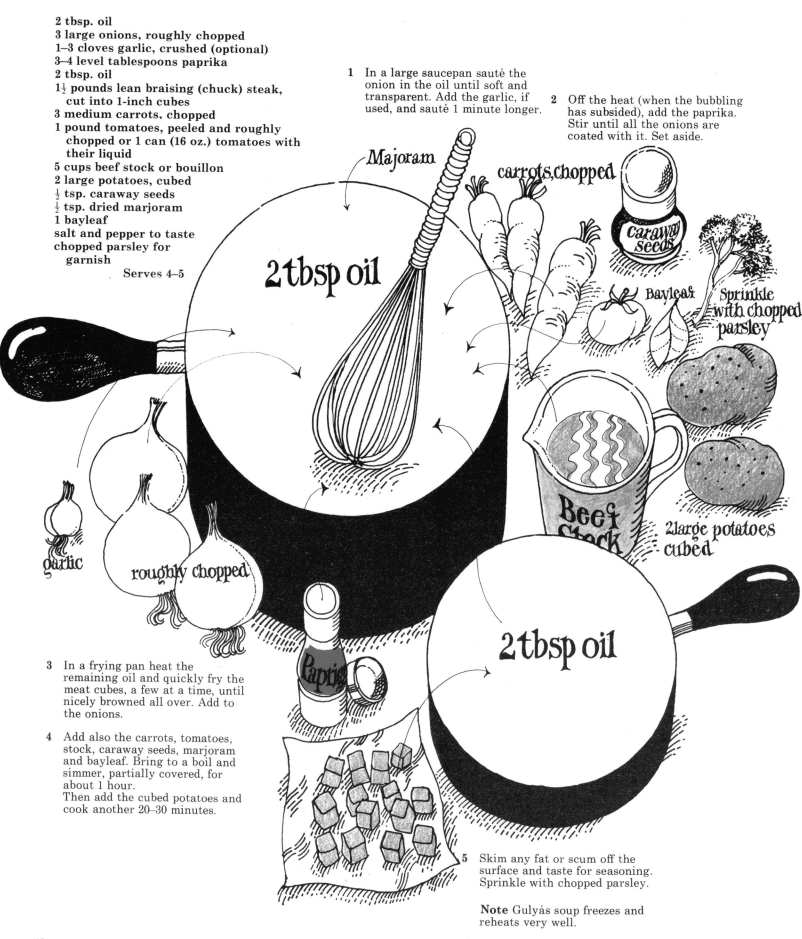

Majoram

2 tbsp oil

carrots, chopped

caraway seeds

Bayleaf

Sprinkle with chopped parsley

Beef Stock

2 large potatoes cubed

garlic

roughly chopped

Paprika

2 tbsp oil

3 In a frying pan heat the remaining oil and quickly fry the meat cubes, a few at a time, until nicely browned all over. Add to the onions.

4 Add also the carrots, tomatoes, stock, caraway seeds, marjoram and bayleaf. Bring to a boil and simmer, partially covered, for about 1 hour.
   Then add the cubed potatoes and cook another 20–30 minutes.

5 Skim any fat or scum off the surface and taste for seasoning. Sprinkle with chopped parsley.

Note Gulyás soup freezes and reheats very well.

HUNGARIAN GULYÁS SOUP

Hungary is famous for its many versions of Gulyás, all hearty, down-to-earth country stews that echo the flavor of Hungarian life. Gulyás soup is born of simple peasant fare and probably evolved as the Magyar tribes roamed central Europe several centuries ago. This soup you will find as colorful and as appetizing to the palate as it is to the eye. Great with a little gypsy music.

2 half chicken breasts
10 cups chicken stock or bouillon
1 large onion, finely chopped
2 medium carrots, finely chopped
2 stalks celery (with leaves
   if possible), finely chopped
1 bayleaf

3 tbsp. butter or margarine
3 tbsp. flour
1–2 tbsp. curry powder
⅜ cup long-grain rice, cooked
salt and pepper to taste
chopped parsley for garnish

Serves 8

3   Sprinkle the vegetables with the flour and
curry powder. Stir well with a wooden
spoon until all the vegetables are coated.
Then, with a wire whisk, stir the vegetables
into the soup pot. Stir well to dissolve the
flour and curry. Bring to a boil and simmer,
partially covered, for 30 minutes.

1   Place the chicken breasts and the stock
or bouillon in a large soup pot. Bring
to a boil, and simmer *very* gently,
partially covered, until chicken
breasts are tender (about 20
minutes). Remove chicken breasts,
and when cool enough to handle,
skin and bone them. Cut the meat
into tiny shreds and reserve.
Leave the cooking liquid in the
soup pot.

Cooked Rice

SALT & PEPPER
CHOPPED PARSLEY
CHICKEN
BREASTS

CHICKEN
Remove & bone

chicken stock

STOCK

4   Add the reserved chicken meat and the
cooked rice and simmer 1 minute longer.

2   In a frying pan sauté the onion, carrot and celery in
the butter for 5 minutes. Then add the bayleaf.

chopped finely

butter

Flour

CURRY POWDER

BAY LEAF

Season to taste with salt and pepper.
Garnish with chopped parsley.
Note This soup reheats very well, and even
freezes.

Mulligatawny

A smooth, succulent, spicy broth. Mulligatawny is a semi-Indian dish, one of many that originated as Dutch, Portuguese, French and English traders ventured to the East. Along with other such curry recipes, it found its way to Europe in the 18th century.

2 pounds cut-up oxtails
4 tbsp. oil
5 tbsp. flour
9 cups beef stock or bouillon
1 onion, chopped
2 carrots, chopped
1 stalk celery, chopped
1 bayleaf
1 tsp. dried thyme or marjoram
1 clove garlic, crushed (optional)
1 large potato, cubed
1 tbsp. tomato puree
salt and pepper to taste
2 tbsp. unsalted butter
2–6 tbsp. dry sherry or Madeira (optional)   Serves 8

1   Sauté the oxtails in the oil until nicely browned all over. Remove and drain on paper towels.

2   To the remaining fat add the flour and stir until the flour has acquired a nice, rich, brown color. (Stir only once in a while, because only the flour on the bottom will color; it needs "turning over" to brown the rest.) Slowly add the stock or bouillon, stirring all the time with a wire whisk. Bring to a boil, skim off the scum and fat, and add the onion, carrot, celery, bayleaf, thyme or marjoram, garlic, potato and tomato purée, and the reserved oxtails. Simmer the soup, partially covered, for 2–3 hours. Skim again if necessary.

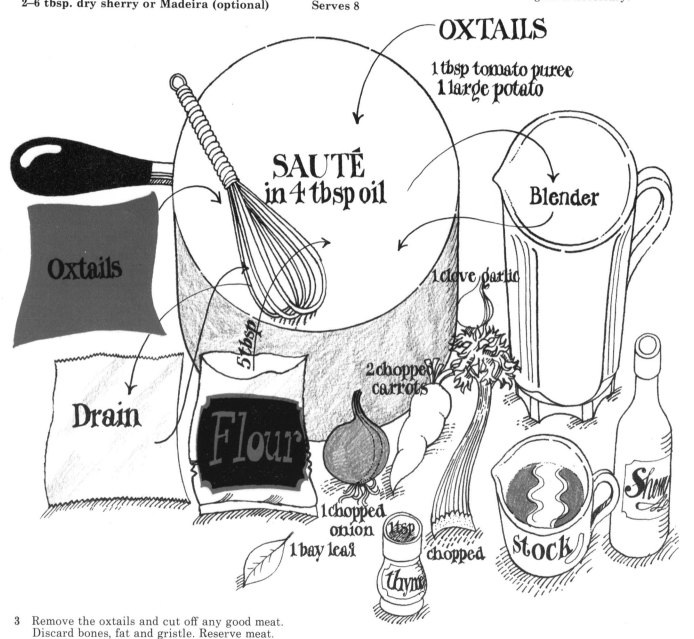

OXTAILS

1 tbsp tomato puree
1 large potato

SAUTÉ in 4 tbsp oil

Blender

1 clove garlic

Oxtails

Drain

Flour

5 tbsp

2 chopped carrots

1 chopped onion
1 bay leaf

1 tsp thyme

chopped

Stock

Sherry

3   Remove the oxtails and cut off any good meat. Discard bones, fat and gristle. Reserve meat.

4   Purée the soup in a blender, return to the soup pot and add the reserved meat to it. Reheat, skimming off any scum and fat that may rise to the surface. Season with salt and pepper.

5   Off the heat, and only just before serving, stir in the soft, unsalted butter and the sherry or Madeira.

Note Can be made ahead or frozen up to stage 4.

Oxtail Soup

It is a little difficult to pin-point the origins of Oxtail Soup. Certainly the ox was one of the earliest of all domesticated animals and as such became part of man's diet, the meat of the ox being used in many ways, one such being soup, as this Chinese poem, dated 3rd century B.C. suggests:

*"Ribs of the fatted ox cooked tender and succulent,
        sour and bitter blended in the soup of Wu."
This soup is delicious, and overdoing the sherry won't hurt a bit!

*(Birch & Keene, *Anthology of Chinese Literature*)

4 tbsp. butter or margarine
1 pound fresh okra, sliced or two
  10-oz. packages frozen okra, sliced
2 tbsp. butter or margarine
1 large onion, chopped
1 green pepper, chopped
1 clove garlic, crushed
2 tbsp. flour
4 cups chicken stock or bouillon
4 tomatoes, skinned, seeded and
  chopped or one 16-oz. can
  tomatoes, well drained and chopped

2 parsley sprigs } tied together
1 bayleaf
½ tsp. dried thyme
salt and pepper to taste
3 or 4 half chicken breasts
2 tbsp. Worcestershire sauce
chopped parsley for garnish

Serves 8

optional:
½ cup rice, cooked
  and hot
½ cup heavy
  cream

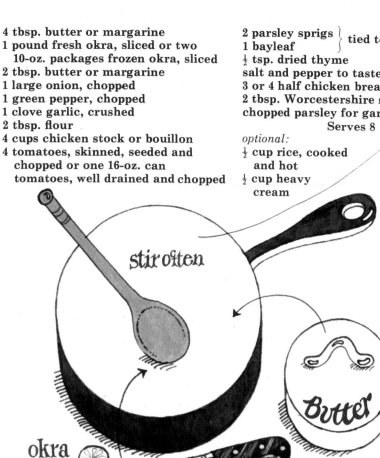

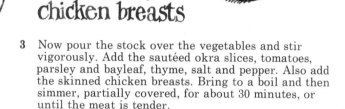

1 In a frying pan melt the butter or margarine. In it sauté the okra slices. Sauté them until the stringiness, that will show itself as white threads due to the heat, disappears. Stir often (cook about 15 minutes). Set aside.

3 Now pour the stock over the vegetables and stir vigorously. Add the sautéed okra slices, tomatoes, parsley and bayleaf, thyme, salt and pepper. Also add the skinned chicken breasts. Bring to a boil and then simmer, partially covered, for about 30 minutes, or until the meat is tender.

4 Remove the chicken and cut the meat into small cubes. Return to pot. Add the Worcestershire sauce and taste for seasoning. Do not boil again!

2 In a soup pot melt the remaining butter. In it sauté the onion and green pepper for 5 minutes, stirring often. Add the garlic and sauté 1 minute longer. Sprinkle the flour over the vegetables. Stir until all of it has been absorbed.

5 Add the cream, if used. If desired, place a tablespoon of hot rice into each soup plate and ladle the soup over it. Sprinkle with parsley.

Note This soup reheats and freezes well.

SOUTHERN CHICKEN GUMBO

chop
chop
chop
chop

1 onion

4 tomatoes
1 pepper

bouillon

Chicken Stock

3 half chicken breasts

bay leaf

1 glove garlic

Okra

2 sprigs parsley

thyme

Gumbos (poultry, meat, fish or shellfish) are typical of Creole cooking with okra added to give the soup its glutinous quality. The soup evolved from a Choctaw Indian dish.

Bon Appetit

1½ pounds soup beef with bone *or*
one 2–3 pound chicken
5 cups cold water
1 tsp. salt
½ tsp. pepper
1 large stalk celery, roughly chopped
1 large carrot, roughly chopped
1 large onion, roughly chopped
2 parsley sprigs
1 bayleaf
½ tsp. dried marjoram
4 tbsp. alphabet noodles, cooked
finely chopped parsley for garnish

Serves 4

1   Place the soup beef (or chicken) in a large saucepan. Add the cold water, salt, pepper, celery, carrot, onion, parsley sprig, bayleaf and marjoram. Bring to a boil and skim if necessary. Simmer the soup, partially covered, 2 hours for beef, 1 hour for chicken. Remove meat or chicken.

2   Strain the soup through a fine-mesh strainer. Discard all the vegetables. Return broth to pot.

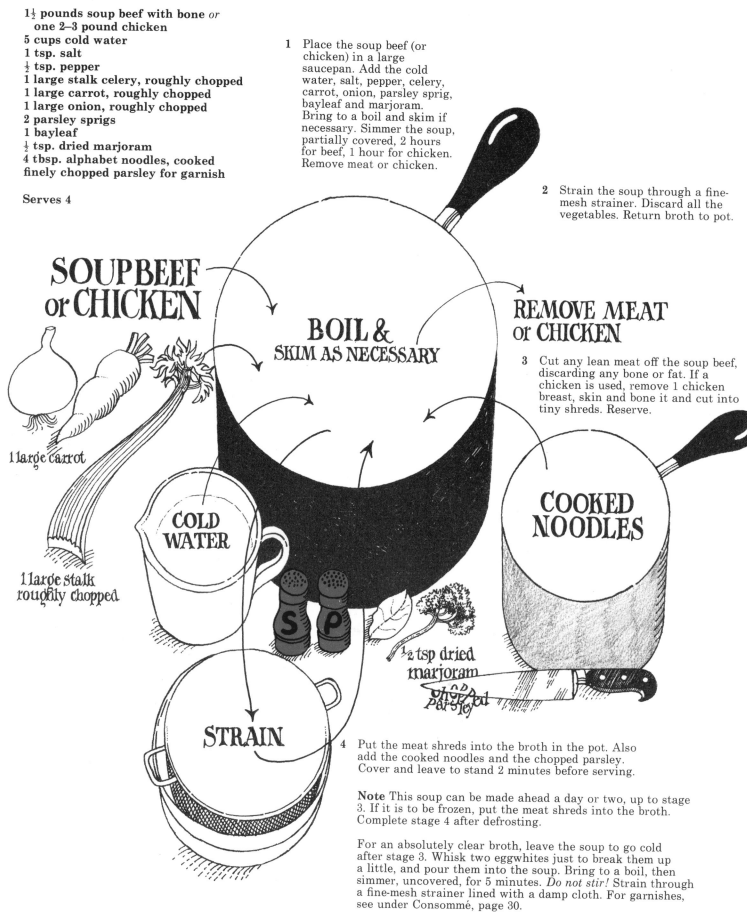

SOUPBEEF or CHICKEN

1 large carrot

1 large stalk roughly chopped

COLD WATER

S P

STRAIN

BOIL & SKIM AS NECESSARY

REMOVE MEAT or CHICKEN

3   Cut any lean meat off the soup beef, discarding any bone or fat. If a chicken is used, remove 1 chicken breast, skin and bone it and cut into tiny shreds. Reserve.

COOKED NOODLES

½ tsp dried marjoram

chopped parsley

4   Put the meat shreds into the broth in the pot. Also add the cooked noodles and the chopped parsley. Cover and leave to stand 2 minutes before serving.

Note This soup can be made ahead a day or two, up to stage 3. If it is to be frozen, put the meat shreds into the broth. Complete stage 4 after defrosting.

For an absolutely clear broth, leave the soup to go cold after stage 3. Whisk two eggwhites just to break them up a little, and pour them into the soup. Bring to a boil, then simmer, uncovered, for 5 minutes. *Do not stir!* Strain through a fine-mesh strainer lined with a damp cloth. For garnishes, see under Consommé, page 30.

FLEISCHBRÜHE

This is an old German soup that has been a hot favorite with countless generations of children. Since its ingredients consist of simple country fare, this recipe or a variation would almost certainly have been popular when Dr. Hoffmann wrote his classic children's story, *Struwwelpeter* in 1844, from which "The Story of Augustus who would not have any soup" is taken. It is a poem that testifies to the importance soup played in a child's diet. Though it is difficult to imagine that this particular soup would have been rejected by Augustus. Ever! This old recipe remains very easy to prepare, is full of nutrition and is a firm favorite with our own children and their friends.

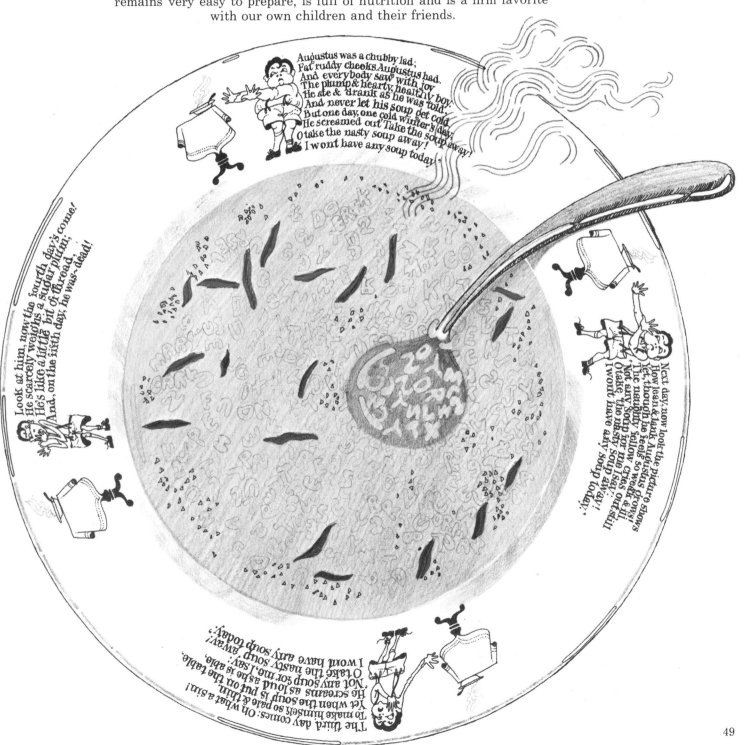

1 package chicken-noodle-soup mix
2 ripe avocados
½ small onion, very finely chopped
1 cup light cream (or half and half)
lemon wedges for garnish
chopped chives for garnish (optional)
juice of ½ lemon (for dipping)
a little salt and pepper if necessary
                                 Serves 4–5

1   Cook the soup mix according to package directions. Leave to cool.

3   Put the cold soup, avocados and onion into blender jar. Blend on low speed for 1 minute, then turn to high and purée the mixture until it is thick and really smooth.

SOUP MIX

water

avocados

CHILL

finely chopped ½ onion

4   Pour into a clean bowl and chill until needed.

5   15 minutes before serving, stir in the cold cream and the reserved avocado slices.

cream

peel & slice

lemon

2   Peel and slice the avocados. Reserve a few of the most perfect slices for garnish. (Dip those for garnish in lemon juice to prevent discoloring.)

6   Garnish with lemon wedges and chopped chives (if used). Taste for seasoning. Serve the same day!

Note Up to stage 4 the soup can be made 2 hours in advance. Do not freeze!

CALIFORNIAN AVOCADO SOUP

A very delicate soup, cool and refined. Ideal for a hot summer's day, this soup makes a superb start to a meal. Surprise and delight your friends with this extraordinary, subtle taste. Escoffier once said "Of all the items on the menu, soup is that which exacts the most delicate perfection and the strictest attention." This soup will stand the closest scrutiny and leave a lasting impression.

1 piece beef for boiling (1½–2 pounds), lean
7 cups beef stock or bouillon
1 marrow bone (optional)
one 1-pound can tomatoes and their juice, chopped
1 stalk celery with leaves, cut into julienne strips
2 sprigs parsley ⎫
2 bay leaves   ⎬ tied together
10 peppercorns ⎭
1 pound green cabbage, shredded
2 medium carrots, cut into julienne strips

2 medium onions, chopped
1 tsp. dried dill
¼ (or less) tsp. caraway seeds
½ cup red wine (optional)
2 tbsp. vinegar
1 tsp. sugar
1 pound cooked beets, fresh or canned (including juice), cut into julienne strips
½ cup sour cream

Serves 5–6

1 Place the meat (and bone, if used) into a large pot. Cover with stock and bring to a boil over high heat. Skim off any scum that rises to the surface. Simmer the meat, partially covered, for about 1 hour. Remove the bone and discard.

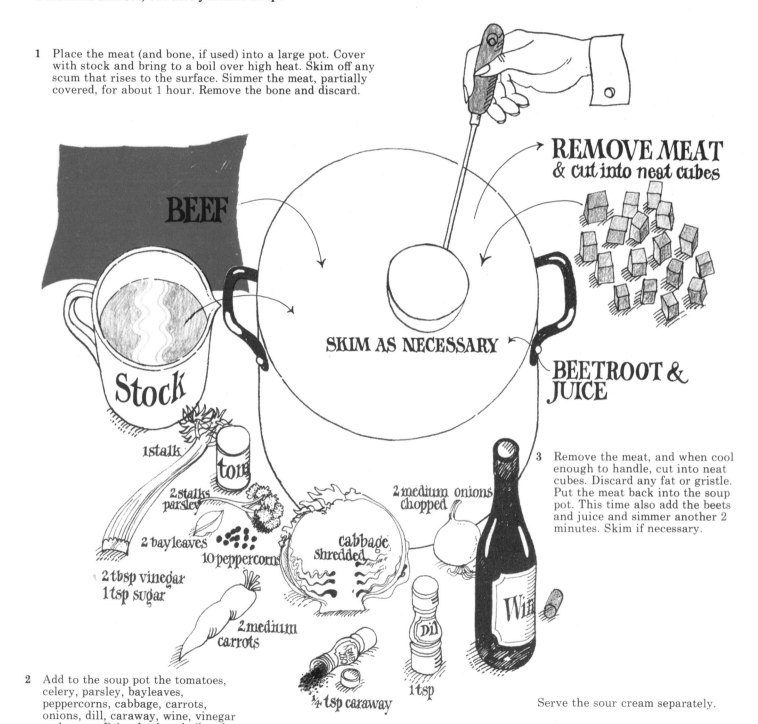

BEEF

Stock

SKIM AS NECESSARY

REMOVE MEAT
& cut into neat cubes

BEETROOT &
JUICE

1 stalk

tom

2 stalks parsley

2 bayleaves

10 peppercorns

2 tbsp vinegar
1 tsp sugar

2 medium carrots

cabbage shredded

2 medium onions chopped

Dil

Win

¼ tsp caraway

1 tsp

3 Remove the meat, and when cool enough to handle, cut into neat cubes. Discard any fat or gristle. Put the meat back into the soup pot. This time also add the beets and juice and simmer another 2 minutes. Skim if necessary.

2 Add to the soup pot the tomatoes, celery, parsley, bayleaves, peppercorns, cabbage, carrots, onions, dill, caraway, wine, vinegar and sugar. Bring back to boil and simmer, partially covered, until the vegetables are tender (30–40 minutes).

Serve the sour cream separately.

Note Borscht improves when reheated. It can also be frozen.

Dill

SOUR CREAM

Caraway

RUSSIAN BORSCHT

RUSSIAN BORSCHT

Borscht is Russia's most famous main-dish soup, full of robust goodness, with an unusual flavor. The addition of beets gives it a gloriously red color which contrasts beautifully with the traditional garnish of sour cream.

53

for the dough
2 cups plain flour
2 large eggs
1 tsp. oil
a little cold water, if needed
for the filling
10 oz. fresh or frozen spinach leaves
1 pound minced pork

1 tsp. dried ground ginger
2 spring onions, finely chopped
1 tsp. oil
3 tsp. soy sauce
salt and pepper to taste
a little dry sherry (optional)
for the soup
6–7 cups hot, well-flavored chicken stock, (*not* bouillon)
a little chopped parsley for garnish
Serves 6–8

1 Cook the spinach leaves in salted water till tender. Drain. Pick out a few nice leaves for garnish and reserve. Put the rest back in the pot, and over a medium heat dry them until all the water has evaporated. Chop finely.

3 Mix together the spinach, pork, ginger, spring onions, oil, soy sauce, salt, pepper and sherry (if used). Mix till well blended.

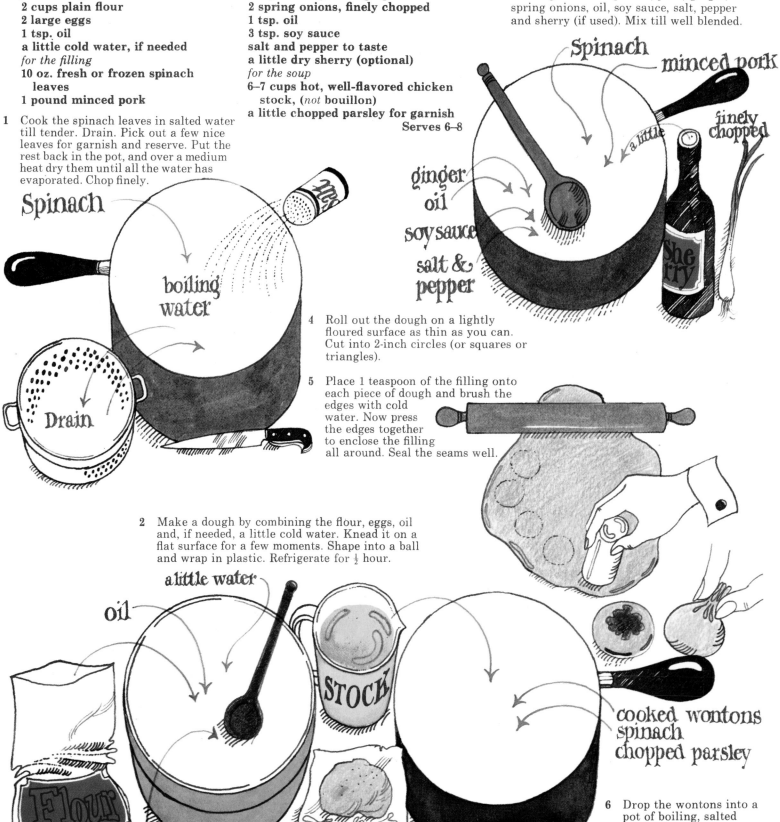

Spinach

boiling water

Drain

ginger
oil
soy sauce
salt & pepper

Spinach

minced pork

a little

finely chopped

Sherry

4 Roll out the dough on a lightly floured surface as thin as you can. Cut into 2-inch circles (or squares or triangles).

5 Place 1 teaspoon of the filling onto each piece of dough and brush the edges with cold water. Now press the edges together to enclose the filling all around. Seal the seams well.

2 Make a dough by combining the flour, eggs, oil and, if needed, a little cold water. Knead it on a flat surface for a few moments. Shape into a ball and wrap in plastic. Refrigerate for ½ hour.

a little water
oil
STOCK
Flour
WRAP & REFRIGERATE

cooked wontons
spinach
chopped parsley

6 Drop the wontons into a pot of boiling, salted water. Simmer them, partially covered, for about 15 minutes.

7 Meanwhile, heat the chicken stock and transfer the cooked wontons to it with a slotted spoon. Also add the reserved spinach leaves.

8 Sprinkle with chopped parsley and serve piping hot.

Note Best when fresh. Soup can be reheated if necessary, but do not freeze.

CHINESE WONTON SOUP

Wonton Soup is a popular main-dish soup from China, a steaming hot broth, with melt-in-the-mouth dumplings filled with a spicy meat mixture. Truly delightful for an informal dinner party.

2–3 pounds chuck steak *or* **pot roast,
tied securely with string**
1 pound chicken backs and necks
11 cups cold water
2 large carrots, chopped
1 medium turnip, chopped
2 leeks, sliced
1 stalk celery, chopped
1 large onion, chopped
2 parsley sprigs } **tied together**
1 large bayleaf
½ tsp. dried thyme
salt and pepper to taste
**1 cut-up marrow bone, tied in a
muslin or cheesecloth bag**

Serves 4

1 Place the beef and chicken backs and necks in a heavy
pot. Pour over the cold water. Bring to a boil over medium
heat. As the scum appears, skim it off, and keep
skimming for several minutes, until the surface is clear.
Now add the vegetables and the bundle of parsley and
bayleaf, the thyme and some salt and pepper.

2 Partially cover the pot and
simmer the soup over the
lowest possible heat. Do
not let it bubble at all at
the sides, cook it really
gently! Simmer for 3
hours.

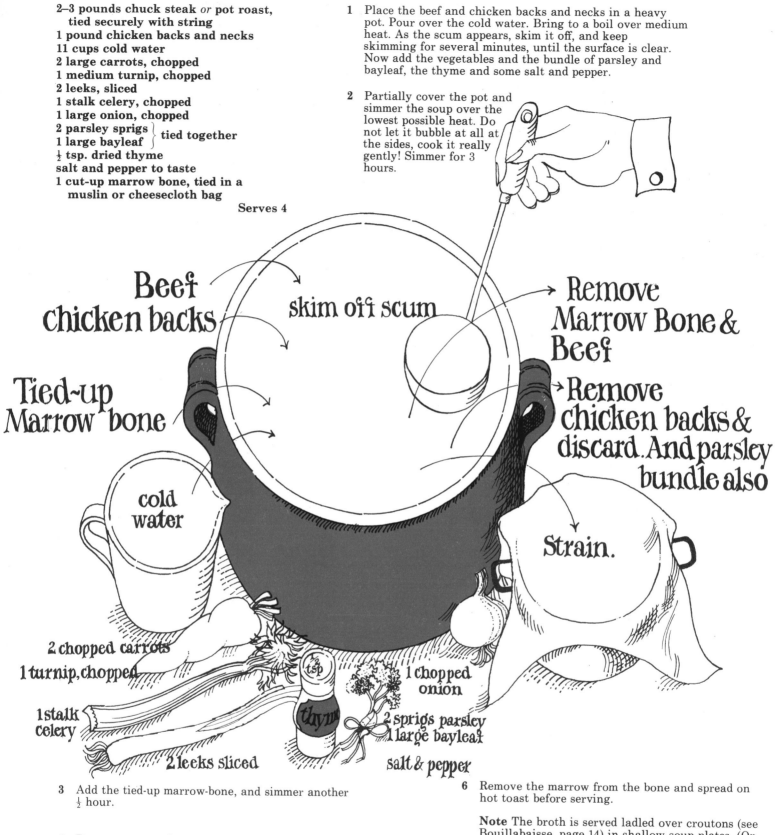

Beef
chicken backs

skim off scum

Remove
Marrow Bone &
Beef

Tied-up
Marrow bone

Remove
chicken backs &
discard. And parsley
bundle also

cold
water

Strain.

2 chopped carrots

1 turnip, chopped

1 stalk
celery

tsp
thyme

1 chopped
onion

2 sprigs parsley
1 large bayleaf

salt & pepper

2 leeks sliced

3 Add the tied-up marrow-bone, and simmer another
½ hour.

4 Remove marrow bone and beef and reserve. Remove chicken
backs and necks and parsley bundle and discard.

5 Strain the broth through a fine-mesh strainer lined with a
damp cloth and discard all the vegetables. Taste the broth
for seasoning and degrease as much as you can.

6 Remove the marrow from the bone and spread on
hot toast before serving.

Note The broth is served ladled over croutons (see
Bouillabaisse, page 14) in shallow soup plates. (Or
use any of the garnishes for clear soups; see
Consommé, page 30.)
The beef is served carved as a second course and
traditionally served with boiled potatoes and
cabbage. And some garnish, like sour gherkins,
coarse salt, mustard, horseradish or tomato sauce.
Reheats well!
Leftover broth freezes well!

POT·AU·FEU

An extremely old French peasant soup of which there are several regional variations. This classic Pot-au-Feu is made of beef and chicken. In some regions of France it is customary to add veal, pork and sometimes mutton.
Like the stockpot, Pot-au-Feu evolved from the cauldron, into which all manner of ingredients were tossed every day. The pot was hung over a fire that was never put out, thus providing an ever-changing broth.

1½ pounds firm, fresh, red cherries
4 whole cloves
1 cinnamon stick or ½ tsp. ground
  cinnamon
juice of 1 lemon
1 piece of lemon rind
4 tbsp. sugar
2 cups cold water
3 tbsp. cornflour
1 glass port or burgundy   **Serves 4**

1   Put the cherries, cloves, cinnamon, lemon juice and lemon
    rind, sugar and water into a soup pot. Bring to a boil
    and simmer, partially covered, until the cherries are
    tender (15–25 minutes).

4   Crack the cherry stones with a sharp blow of a hammer
    and place them in a small saucepan. Add the port or
    burgundy, bring to a boil – then remove from heat, cover,
    and leave to infuse for 15–20 minutes. Strain through a
    fine-mesh strainer and reserve the liquid. Discard stones.

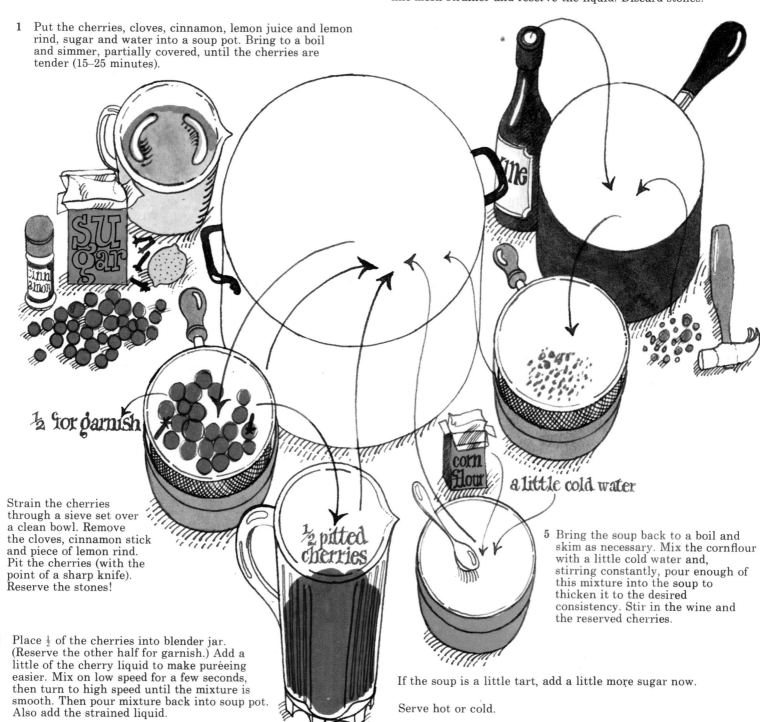

½ for garnish

½ pitted cherries

a little cold water

2   Strain the cherries
    through a sieve set over
    a clean bowl. Remove
    the cloves, cinnamon stick
    and piece of lemon rind.
    Pit the cherries (with the
    point of a sharp knife).
    Reserve the stones!

5   Bring the soup back to a boil and
    skim as necessary. Mix the cornflour
    with a little cold water and,
    stirring constantly, pour enough of
    this mixture into the soup to
    thicken it to the desired
    consistency. Stir in the wine and
    the reserved cherries.

3   Place ½ of the cherries into blender jar.
    (Reserve the other half for garnish.) Add a
    little of the cherry liquid to make puréeing
    easier. Mix on low speed for a few seconds,
    then turn to high speed until the mixture is
    smooth. Then pour mixture back into soup pot.
    Also add the strained liquid.

If the soup is a little tart, add a little more sugar now.

Serve hot or cold.

Note If the soup is to be eaten cold and it has thickened too
much, thin it down with a little port or burgundy. Eat same day!
Blueberries can be substituted for the cherries.

KIRSCHSUPPE

A magnificent German soup. Absolutely delicious – try this soup when cherries are in season. It's a special summer flavor typical of German cooking – with a taste you can't afford to miss!

5 tbsp sugar
1 small piece lemon peel
½ tsp. powdered cinnamon
2 cloves
1½ cups milk
one 12-oz. can dark or lager beer
4 tbsp. cornflour
½ cup heavy cream
1 egg yolk
1 tbsp. brandy (optional)
1 egg white (optional)

Serves 4

1 Place sugar, lemon peel, cinnamon and cloves in heavy saucepan. Pour over the milk and beer. Leave uncovered and bring to a boil, stirring a little so as not to burn the sugar.

2 Mix the cornflour with enough water to make a smooth pouring consistency, and pour enough of this into the soup (stirring all the time with a wire whisk) to reach the desired thickness. The soup should be just thickened enough to coat the back of a spoon. Boil for just half a minute. Remove from heat.

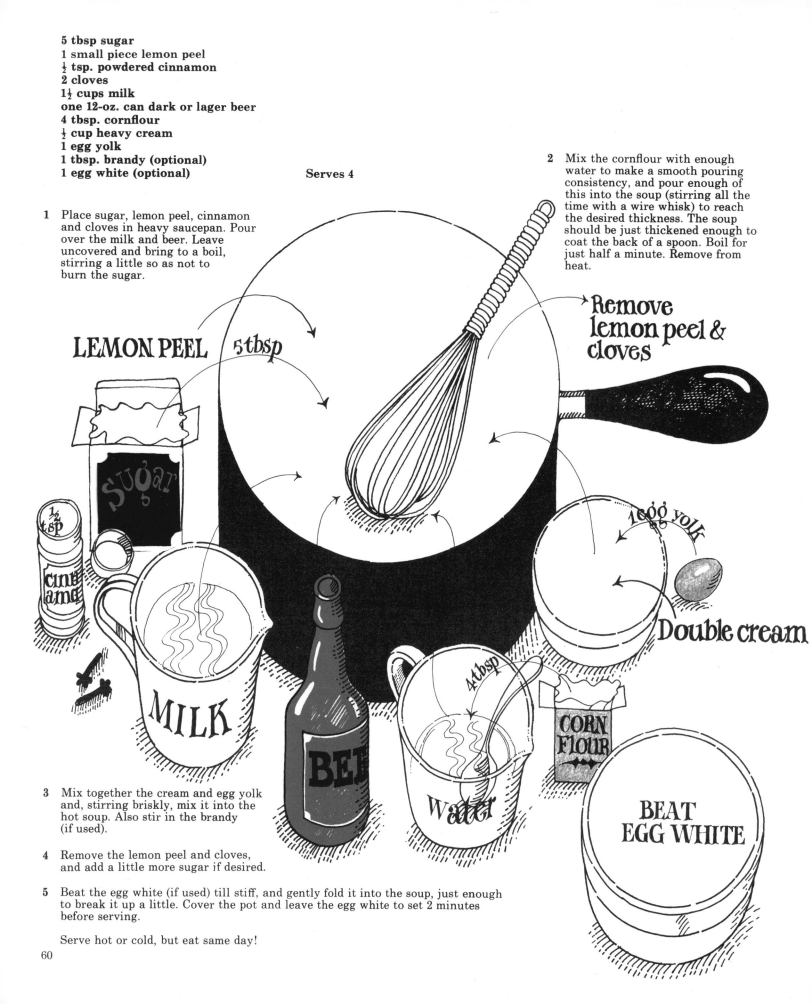

LEMON PEEL

5 tbsp

Remove lemon peel & cloves

sugar

½ tsp

cinnamon

MILK

BEER

4 tbsp

Water

CORN FLOUR

1 egg yolk

Double cream

BEAT EGG WHITE

3 Mix together the cream and egg yolk and, stirring briskly, mix it into the hot soup. Also stir in the brandy (if used).

4 Remove the lemon peel and cloves, and add a little more sugar if desired.

5 Beat the egg white (if used) till stiff, and gently fold it into the soup, just enough to break it up a little. Cover the pot and leave the egg white to set 2 minutes before serving.

Serve hot or cold, but eat same day!

Biersuppe

Guten Appetit

Biersuppe is a typically German soup, that in all probability dates back several centuries. It is further testimony to the German love of beer. In Germany, it is usually made with dark beer, which has a very low alcohol content. Mostly it is eaten hot, usually preceding a cold evening meal. When made with lager beer, it is best eaten well chilled.

STOCKS

Beef Stock

5–6 pounds beef bones (shin and marrow mixture)
2 pigs feet, split in half
4 quarts cold water
½ pound carrots, chopped
½ pound onions, chopped
2 stalks celery, chopped
2 parsley sprigs ⎞
1 bayleaf ⎠ tied together
1 tsp. dried thyme

Place the bones and pigs feet into a large pot. Cover them with the cold water.

Bring the pot to a boil over high heat. As the scum appears on the surface, skim it off (see under Skimming, page 6). Keep skimming it for about 30 minutes, until the scum ceases to rise. (You don't have to be too careful at this point, most of the liquid being scooped up is water.) Now add the chopped vegetables and the bouquet garnie and simmer the stock, only partially covered, for 8 hours.

Strain the stock through a damp cloth set in a sieve over a large pot or pail. Discard the bones and vegetables.

Store the stock in individual 1-pint containers. It can be refrigerated for about 2 weeks, or frozen for months.

Chicken Stock

4–5 pounds chicken backs and necks
4 quarts cold water
½ pound carrots, chopped
½ pound onions, chopped
2 stalks celery, chopped
2 parsley sprigs ⎞
1 bayleaf ⎠ tied together
½ tsp. dried thyme

Place the chicken backs and necks into a large pot. Cover them with the cold water.

Bring to a boil. As the scum appears on the surface, skim it off. Keep skimming until the scum no longer appears. (See under beef stock.)

Add the cut-up vegetables and the bouquet garni and simmer, partially covered, for 5 hours.

Strain and store as for beef stock.

Fish Stock

1 medium carrot, chopped
1 medium onion, chopped
1 stalk celery, chopped
1 bayleaf ⎞
2 parsley sprigs ⎠ tied together
½ tsp. dried thyme
2 pints cold water
2 pints dry white wine
3 pounds heads and tails of white fish

Place all ingredients in a large pot. Bring to a boil. As the scum appears, skim it off very carefully. (You don't want to waste any of the wine!) Skim until the scum no longer appears, otherwise the stock will be cloudy.

Simmer the stock, partially covered, about 1 hour.

Strain and store as for beef stock.

INDEX